THE DIRT BOOK

POEMS ABOUT ANIMALS
THAT LIVE BENEATH OUR FEET

by DAVID L. HARRISON   *illustrated by* KATE COSGROVE

HOLIDAY HOUSE • NEW YORK

To Allen and Lisa Wakefield with love —D.L.H.

For my mom, Marsha, who gave me the courage to peek
under rocks and endless jars to fill with bugs —K.C.

The publisher thanks Robert Kipfer, Springfield Plateau Chapter,
Missouri Master Naturalists, for his expert review of this book.

Text copyright © 2021 by David L. Harrison
Illustrations copyright © 2021 by Kate Cosgrove
All Rights Reserved
HOLIDAY HOUSE is registered in the U.S. Patent and Trademark Office.
Printed and bound in October 2022 at Toppan Leefung, DongGuan, China.
The artwork was created with colored pencils and digital tools.
www.holidayhouse.com
First Edition
5 7 9 10 8 6 4

Library of Congress Cataloging-in-Publication Data

Names: Harrison, David L. (David Lee), 1937–author.
Cosgrove, Kate, illustrator.
Title: The dirt book : poems about animals that live beneath our feet
poems by David L. Harrison ; illustrations by Kate Cosgrove.
Description: First edition. || New York : Holiday House, [2021]
Includes notes about dirt and the organisms that live in it.
Includes bibliographical references. || Audience: Ages 5–9.
Audience: Grades 2–3. || Summary: "A collection of poems about dirt and the many organisms
that live there such as grubs, trapdoor spiders, moles, earthworms, chipmunks, and doodlebugs"
— Provided by publisher. || Identifiers: LCCN 2020009970 || ISBN 9780823438617 (hardcover)
Subjects: LCSH: Soils—Juvenile poetry. || Soil animals—Juvenile poetry.
Children's poetry, American. || CYAC: Soils—Poetry. || Soil animals—Poetry. || American poetry. || LCGFT: Poetry.
Classification: LCC PS3558.A6657 D57 2021 || DDC 811/.54—dc23
LC record available at https://lccn.loc.gov/2020009970
ISBN: 978-0-8234-3861-7 (hardcover)

CONTENTS

THIS BOOK IS ABOUT DIRT

We get dirt on our pants.
Under our fingernails.
In our hair.

Wet dirt helps mud dauber
wasps stick their houses onto
our houses. Dry dirt makes us
sneeze on windy days.

Dirt seems to be everywhere,
but there's less of it than you
might think. Oceans, lakes,
and rivers cover much of our
planet. Most of what's left is
too rainy or dry or rocky or
sandy or steep or hot or cold to
support much dirt.

The first dirt was formed
almost four billion years ago
when Earth was young,
but most of it may be less
than two million years old.
More dirt is being made all the
time, but it can take hundreds of
years to make a layer one inch deep.

What is dirt anyway?
Where does it come from?
What's in it? What's down
there? Are there things down
there creeping, crawling,
sleeping, and growing in the
dark where not the tiniest pinhole
of light can ever reach? If we could
ride a magic elevator straight down
into the world beneath our feet,
what do you think we'd see?
When you turn the page, you
are going to find out.

DIRT RECIPE

Grind up . . .

flakes cracked from rocks
and chipped by prying roots.

Add dead things . . .

like rotting leaves,
bees, decaying shoots.

Mix with . . .

maggots, beetles, mites,
centipedes, worms.

Serves . . .

a host of hungry fungi
and at least a billion germs.

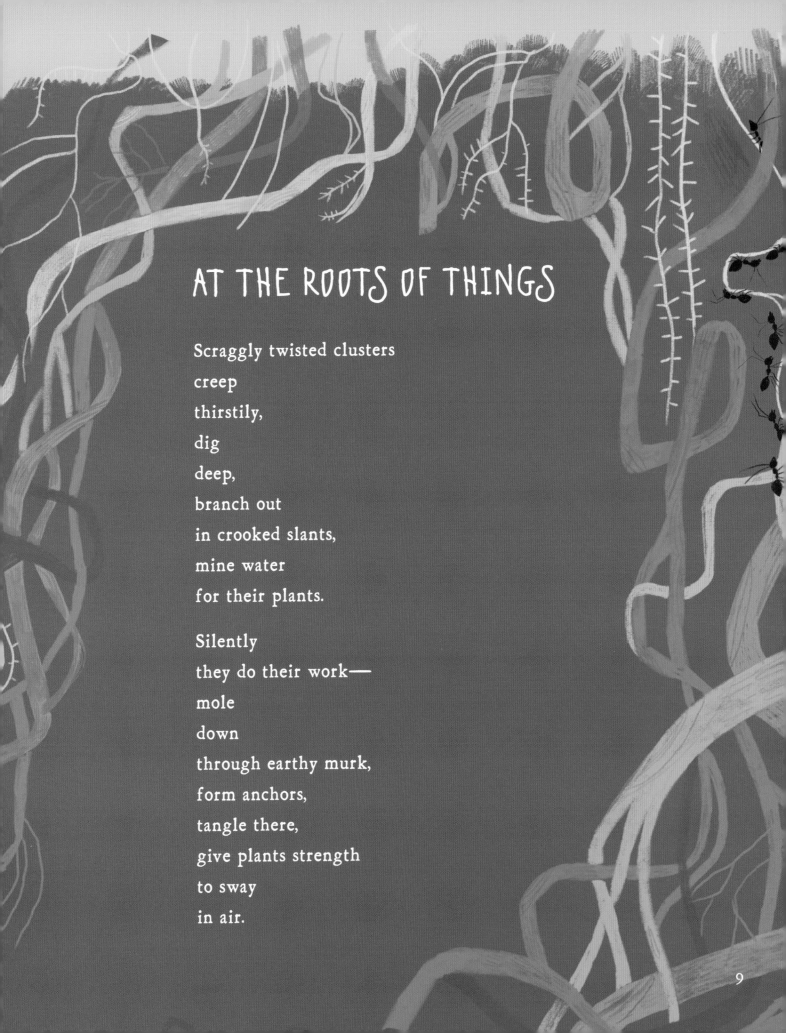

AT THE ROOTS OF THINGS

Scraggly twisted clusters
creep
thirstily,
dig
deep,
branch out
in crooked slants,
mine water
for their plants.

Silently
they do their work—
mole
down
through earthy murk,
form anchors,
tangle there,
give plants strength
to sway
in air.

DOODLEBUG
ONE-WAY RIDE

Doodlebug, doodlebug fashions a
funnel so innocent looking, yet
be there no doubt about all
of the ants that will come
slippy-sliding till
doodlebug greets
them, and none
will get
out.

TRAPDOOR SPIDER
THE WAITING GAME

Lurks in hidden buried lair—
mo
   tion
      less
         ly—
for the unaware cricket,
centipede,
roach . . .

waits,
watches it approach,

opens the door,
leaps,

and zap!

Another meal
goes
down
the
trap.

EARTHWORM
DIRTY WORK

Earthworm squiggles,
earthworm squirms,
earthworm dines on
dirt and germs.

Earthworm dodges,
earthworm weaves,
earthworm nibbles
dead wet leaves.

Earthworm crawls,
earthworm creeps,
earthworm tunnels,
rarely sleeps.

ANT
CITY BUILDER

A thousand ants, without a sound,
build a city underground.
Without light, they build halls.
Down and down the city sprawls.
Without rest, they tug and toil,
grain by grain, remove soil.
Without a leader in the gloom,
they scoop and hollow out each room.
Without tools, they clean and sweep,
and build their city strong and deep.

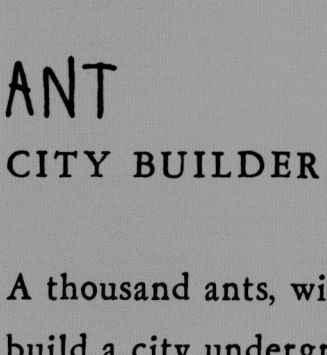

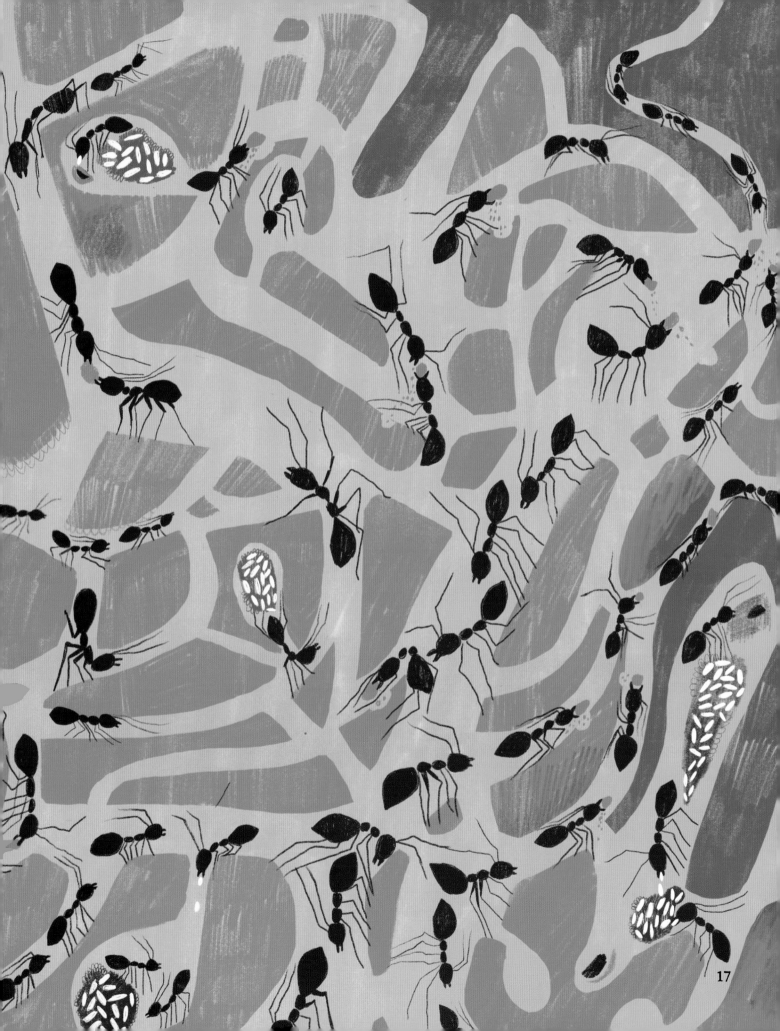

GRUB
GRASS KILLER

Down in the grass,
down in the soil,
down in the roots—
   grubs spoil.

Down in the dark,
down in the dirt,
down in the silence—
   grub alert!

MOUSE
NIGHTFALL CALLS

Below the doodlebugs
and grubs—
still farther down—
a small brown ball of fur
stirs, rests,
digesting last night's berry,
insect, seed,
needs to rouse from sleep,
creep through steep halls
as nightfall
calls it from its tunneled home
to venture out,
to roam.

BUMBLEBEE
PLANNING FOR SPRING

When autumn comes to fold the flowers,
the queen needs a place to rest
so she can live to build a nest
when spring returns with sunny hours.

With a low bumble-buzzing sound
she digs a hole where she can creep,
settles down and falls asleep,
snug and cozy underground.

YELLOW JACKET WASP

WARNING! WARNING! WARNING!

Inside that nest
inside that hole
inside the ground
are found
a thousand warnings
to go around.

MOLE
WORM SEARCH

Ridges, mounds, tunnels, holes—
    earthworm-gobbling hungry moles.
Ridges, mounds, tunnels, holes—
    handiwork of tiny trolls,
    furry demons on patrol,
    working where it's black as coal.
    Tracking down a worm's the goal
    of every tiny mole troll soul.
Ridges, mounds, tunnels, holes—
    earthworm-gobbling hungry moles.

TOAD
BEDTIME

Above ground the leaves pile deep
as toad begins to claw and creep
down through dirt to make a nest
where it can take its winter rest.
Time, now, for toad to sleep.

CHIPMUNK
BUSY, BUSY, BUSY!

Chipmunk, for such a little squirt
you sure do move a lot of dirt,
you sure do dig your tunnels deep,
you sure do find some nuts to keep,
you sure do know your underground.
Chipmunk, you sure do get around.

31

GOPHER TORTOISE
THE INN KEEPER

The gopher tortoise has a lot of guests.
He never knows who might show up today.
He never shows them if he thinks they're pests.

Patiently he walks around their nests,
gently moves some bunnies in his way.
He never shows them if he thinks they're pests.

Skunks and foxes have to pass a test.
They know they must behave if they're to stay.
The gopher tortoise has a lot of guests.

The gopher tortoise never seems distressed
when someone else moves in while he's away.
He never shows them if he thinks they're pests.

The gopher tortoise always does his best
to go about his business come what may.
The gopher tortoise has a lot of guests.

Perhaps the gopher tortoise thinks he's blessed.
It could be he's content, but who can say?
The gopher tortoise has a lot of guests.
He never shows them if he thinks they're pests.

AND NOW WE KNOW

Beneath our feet, beyond our sight,
below the roots where green grass grows,
there's more to dirt than we'd suppose.
In places black as blackest night,
creatures slither, wriggle, creep,
nurse their babies, snuggle, sleep—
There's more to dirt than we'd suppose.

Quiet things in hidden holes
burrow down where secrets lie.
There's more to dirt than meets the eye.
From centipedes to mousy voles
they come and go without a sound,
seek their safety underground—
There's more to dirt than meets the eye.

Creatures large and small retreat
where boulders rest and tree roots drink.
There's more to dirt than we might think.
So many lives beneath our feet,
so much to learn, so much to know—
And now we've learned a lot, although
there's more to dirt than we might think.

AUTHOR NOTES

DIRT

Did you know that rain and roots help make dirt? Water seeping through the soil softens the earth around buried rocks. As the rocks shift and grind, tiny flakes chip off. Thirsty tree roots probing for water press against the rocks and break off more chips. Mix billions of rock flakes with humus (HEW-mus) and you get dirt. And what is humus? It's the decaying remains of plants and animals and the billions of miniature scavengers that feed on them, a regular zoo of fungi (FUN-ji), worms, bacteria, mites, and insects that grub, grope, and gobble through the gritty underworld.

ROOTS

Roots come in many shapes and sizes. Some grow down like stalactites. Others look like chin whiskers. If you see carrots, radishes, onions, beets, and turnips, you're under a garden. They're roots too. Tasty ones! Grass roots grow four or five inches deep, while tree roots reach three to six feet and a few run far deeper. All roots perform important work. They soak up water and minerals from the soil to feed the plant. Next time you see limbs swaying in the wind, be glad for those strong roots that keep the tree from blowing over!

DOODLEBUG

If you look around in sandy soil on a warm day, you might see funnel-shaped traps of doodlebugs. Chances are that hungry doodlebugs are hiding under the sand at the bottoms of the holes. With pinchers open, doodlebugs wait patiently for an unfortunate ant or other small insect to come tumbling down the steep walls and into their clutches. A doodlebug is the baby form (larva) of a flying insect called the ant lion. This stage may last two to three years.

TRAPDOOR SPIDER

The trapdoor spider digs a hole several inches deep, wide enough for it to turn around in. It lines the walls with silk and covers the trap with a door constructed from bits of leaves, fungi, and soil held together with silk threads and hinged on one side. The hidden spider waits for a small creature to venture too close, then rushes out to ambush its next meal. Its mortal enemy is the spider wasp. The wasp stings and paralyzes the spider and lays an egg on it. When the wasp larva hatches, the spider becomes it first meal.

EARTHWORM

The earthworm is one of the most valuable creatures on Earth. It's an eating machine that likes dead leaves, decaying animals, and manure. What goes in may not be appealing, but what comes out helps plants grow. The earthworm tunnels into the ground by eating its way through the soil. The holes it makes provide spaces for air and rainwater to flow into the ground and make it richer. An acre of soil can have a million worms in it. After birds, snakes, foxes, moles, and fishermen take their toll, plenty of worms are left to do their dirty work.

ANT

If you've seen red ants and black ants and think that's it, think again. Scientists have identified more than 12,000 kinds and believe they'll find more. Small colonies may have a few hundred members, but some colonies are so huge they have more than one million. Like their bee cousins, ant communities rely on queens to lay the eggs and females to do the work. Males are needed for mating with new queens but otherwise don't do much or live long. Ants like fruit, dead things, and many kinds of human food. That seems fair. In some countries, people eat ants.

GRUB

A grub looks like a sturdy, dirty-white caterpillar with a brown head. But it isn't a caterpillar, and it won't grow up to become a butterfly or moth. A grub is a baby Japanese beetle. Birds, moles, and skunks love to eat grubs, but people don't. Grubs tunnel under lawns and kill grass by eating the roots. Grubs munch away down there in the dark until winter, and then they dig down deeper until summer. When they've finished growing up, they crawl out of the ground as beetles and spend the rest of their short, hungry lives ruining our roses and grapes.

MOUSE

Mice are good at three things: making more mice, eating, and hiding. They start having babies before they're two months old and can have more every month after that. One pair and their children can produce thousands of mice in one year! They're not picky eaters and nibble off and on all night at fruit, grain, seeds, even meat. By day many mice hole up in underground tunnels where they're snug and safe from cats, foxes, and other animals that like mouse meat. When the weather turns cold, they stay down there and don't move around much.

BUMBLEBEE

Late in the year, when plant blossoms begin to fade, a new bumblebee queen flies from the nest and finds a mate. After that she fattens up on enough pollen and nectar to last for months. When she's ready, she searches for a safe place to pass the winter. She may dig under a shed or make a hole in the ground or move into an empty mouse tunnel. The other bumblebees in her colony perish during the winter, but the queen lives on. In the spring she comes out, builds a new nest, lays eggs, and starts a new colony.

YELLOW JACKET WASP

Down in the ground we sometimes find a cousin of the bumblebee—the yellow jacket. These testy wasps are quick to swarm out and go to war with people or animals that come too near the opening to their underground lair. As much as four feet below ground, in a hole they've found or dug themselves, the wasps build their paper-like nest of chewed wood fiber mixed with saliva. Yellow jacket nests can be as big as a basketball and home to thousands of wasps. They should hang out a sign: LEAVE US ALONE! Or maybe: BUZZ OFF!

MOLE

When a mole needs a worm snack, it digs after one lickety-split. A hungry mole can tunnel its way across your garden just below the surface as fast as fifteen feet per hour. If it runs across grubs and snails and slugs along the way, it gobbles them too. The mole's digging tears up lawn and garden plant roots, which is why it's so unpopular with people. And that's not all. Farther down, one or two feet below its food-gathering tunnels, the mole digs more tunnels to help it get from one good hunting spot to another quicker.

TOAD

A toad egg hatches in the water, and the tadpole lives there until it loses its tail, grows legs, and hops onto land. There the toad spends the rest of its life eating worms, slugs, and thousands of insects each year. But a toad doesn't always live above ground. In places with cold winters, it spends part of the year living below ground where it digs into the dirt to hide itself and to keep warm, sometimes as deep as three feet into the earth. There it falls into a deep sleep called "hibernation" and waits for the bugs of spring to return.

CHIPMUNK

These small members of the squirrel family are good climbers but they like life better on the ground and below it. Mornings and evenings they stay busy stuffing their cheeks with nuts, berries, and seeds and dashing home to feast on some and store the rest. A chipmunk home is a series of tunnels, some as long as thirty feet and buried three feet deep. Here and there are chambers for extra food to save for winter. The nursery is an important place where newborn babies can be safe until they are old enough to crawl out and meet the world.

GOPHER TORTOISE

If the dirt is sandy enough, one of the biggest tunnels below us will be made by a gopher tortoise. With its shovel-like front legs and strong back legs, it digs tunnels that run on for forty feet or longer and can be more than ten feet deep. The gopher tortoise is so gentle that hundreds of other kinds of animals have been spotted borrowing space for themselves. We might see anything from mice, frogs, crickets, and snakes to foxes, skunks, opossums, rabbits—even owls. In the case of a forest fire, a lot of them may show up at once!

BIBLIOGRAPHY

DIRT

1. "How Is Dirt Made?" by Larry Scheckel, Mother Earth News, June 2018; https://www.motherearthnews.com/nature-and-environment/nature/how-dirt-made-ze0z1806zcoy.
2. "One Amazing Substance Allowed Life to Thrive on Land," by Claire Asher; BBC, December 5, 2015; http://www.bbc.com/earth/story/20151205-one-amazing-substance-allowed-life-to-thrive-on-land.
3. "Welcome to Soil-net.com," accessed December 5, 2014; http://www.soil-net.com/dev/page.cfm?pageid=secondary_intro&loginas=anon_secondary.

ROOTS

1. "Root," by the editors of Encyclopaedia Britannica, updated March 25, 2020; https://www.britannica.com/science/root-plant.
2. "Plant Roots," from Basic Biology, edited by Adam Purcell, last edited January 18, 2016; https://basicbiology.net/plants/physiology/roots.
3. "Plant Parts," Missouri Botanical Gardens, accessed November 24, 2014; http://www.mbgnet.net/bioplants/parts.html.

DOODLEBUG

1. "What does a doodlebug, doodlebug do all day?" by Karen Benson, Beeville Bee-Picayune, July 1, 2018; https://www.mysoutex.com/beeville_bee_picayune/news/features/what-does-a-doodlebug-doodlebug-do-all-day/article_6988b656-7628-11e8-b13b-5b83b660c7ad.html.
2. "Antlion Larvae (Doodlebug Larvae)," Missouri Department of Conservation, accessed December 8, 2014; https://nature.mdc.mo.gov/discover-nature/field-guide/antlion-larvae-doodlebug-larvae.
3. "Antlions and Doodlebugs," Iowa State University Extension and Outreach; https://hortnews.extension.iastate.edu/antlions-and-doodlebugs

TRAPDOOR SPIDER

1. "Trap-door Spider," by the editors of Encyclopaedia Britannica, updated February 23, 2020; https://www.britannica.com/animal/trap-door-spider.
2. "Trapdoor Spider," Animal Corner, accessed December 8, 2014; https://animalcorner.org/animals/trapdoor-spider.
3. "Trapdoor Spider, Ummidia spp.," Arizona-Sonora Desert Museum, accessed December 8, 2014; http://www.desertmuseum.org/books/nhsd_trapdoor_spider.php.

EARTHWORM

1. "Common Earthworm," National Geographic, accessed December 2, 2014; https://www.nationalgeographic.com/animals/invertebrates/c/common-earthworm.
2. "Earthworms," The National Wildlife Federation, accessed December 2, 2014; https://www.nwf.org/Educational-Resources/Wildlife-Guide/Invertebrates/Earthworms.
3. "The Living Soil: Earthworms," by Clive A. Edwards, United States Department of Agriculture: Natural Resources Conservation Service, accessed December 2, 2014; https://www.nrcs.usda.gov/wps/portal/nrcs/detailfull/soils/health/biology/?cid=nrcs142p2_053863.

ANT

1. "Ants," National Geographic, accessed December 8, 2014; https://www.nationalgeographic.com/animals/invertebrates/group/ants.
2. "Ants," University of Minnesota Extension, Jeffrey Hahn and Phillip Pellitteri; https://extension.umn.edu/insects-infest-homes/ants.
3. "Ants," by the editors of Encyclopaedia Britannica, updated May 20, 2020; https://www.britannica.com/animal/ant.

GRUB

1. "Featured Creatures: White Grubs," by Lane Selman, University of Florida IFAS; http://entnemdept.ufl.edu/creatures/field/white_grub.htm.
2. "How to Identify Nematodes and Garden Grubs," by Kristi Waterworth for SFGate, accessed September 13, 2016; https://homeguides.sfgate.com/identify-nematodes-garden-grubs-47986.html.

MOUSE

1. "House mouse or field mouse? A quick guide to types of mice, voles and shrews in the UK," by Helen Keating, Woodland Trust, January 21, 2019; https://www.woodlandtrust.org.uk/blog/2019/01/types-of-uk-mice/.
2. "Mouse Facts: Habits, Habitat & Types of Mice," by Alina Bradford, Live Science, June 26, 2014; https://www.livescience.com/28028-mice.html.
3. "The Difference Between Rats and Mice and Why It Matters," by Lisa Jo Lupo, The Spruce, updated January 7, 2020; https://www.thespruce.com/the-difference-between-rats-and-mice-2656563.

BUMBLEBEE

1. "Facts About Bumblebees," by Alina Bradford, Live Science, January 14, 2017; https://www.livescience.com/57509-bumblebee-facts.html.

2. "Bumblebee," Washington Nature Mapping Program, accessed September 14, 2016; http://naturemappingfoundation.org/natmap/facts/bumblebee_k6.html.

3. "5 Facts About Bumble Bees—and How To Help Them," by Laura Tangley, National Wildlife Federation blog, April 26, 2014; https://blog.nwf.org/2014/04/5-facts-about-bumble-bees-and-how-to-help-them.

YELLOW JACKET WASP

1. "Yellow Jacket," Washington Nature Mapping Program, accessed September 15, 2016; http://naturemappingfoundation.org/natmap/facts/yellow_jacket_712.html.

2. "Featured Creatures: Yellowjackets and Hornets," by E. E. Grissell, University of Florida IFAS; http://entnemdept.ufl.edu/creatures/urban/occas/hornet_yellowjacket.htm.

MOLE

1. "Facts About Moles," by Alina Bradford, Live Science, September 25, 2015; https://www.livescience.com/52297-moles.html.

2. "Moles," National Wildlife Federation, accessed September 15, 2016; https://www.nwf.org/Educational-Resources/Wildlife-Guide/Mammals/Moles.

3. "Mole," by Guy Musser, Encylopaedia Britannica, updated March 4, 2020; https://www.britannica.com/animal/mole-mammal.

TOAD

1. "Toad," by the editors of Encyclopaedia Britannica, updated October 25, 2018; https://www.britannica.com/animal/toad.

2. "Toads," National Wildlife Federation, accessed September 16, 2016; https://www.nwf.org/Educational-Resources/Wildlife-Guide/Amphibians/Toads.

3. "Five Facts that Will Make You Like Toads," by Kiley, Dickinson County Conservation Board, June 4, 2018; https://dickinsoncountyconservationboard.com/2018/06/04/five-facts-that-will-make-you-like-toads.

CHIPMUNK

1. "Chipmunks," National Geographic, accessed September 16, 2016; https://www.nationalgeographic.com/animals/mammals/group/chipmunks.

2. "10 Things You Don't Know About Chipmunks," by Sidney Stevens, Treehugger, updated November 7, 2019; https://www.treehugger.com/things-you-dont-know-about-chipmunks-4864283.

3. "NOT Alvin and the Chipmunks: 10 Facts You May Not Know about the Real Rodents," by Roger Di Silvestro, National Wildlife Federation blog, December 13, 2011; https://blog.nwf.org/2011/12/not-alvin-and-the-chipmunks-10-facts-about-the-real-rodents.

GOPHER TORTOISE

1. "Gopher Tortoise," Florida Fish and Wildlife Conservation Commission, accessed September 16, 2016; https://myfwc.com/wildlifehabitats/profiles/reptiles/gopher-tortoise.

2. "Gopher Tortoise," National Geographic, accessed September 1, 2016; https://www.nationalgeographic.com/animals/reptiles/g/gopher-tortoise.